D

Dave Mirra

By Jeff Savage

Lerner Publications Company • Minneapolis

Para mi hijo Mario Llamas—fearless, future gold medal superstar

Text copyright © 2007 by Jeff Savage

Lerner Publications Company
A division of Lerner Publishing Group
241 First Avenue North
Minneapolis, MN 55401 U.S.A.

Website address: www.lernerbooks.com

Library of Congress Cataloging-in-Publication Data

Savage, Jeff, 1961–
    Dave Mirra / by Jeff Savage.
      p.   cm. —(Amazing athletes)
    Includes index.
    ISBN-13: 978–0–8225–6593–2 (lib. bdg. : alk. paper)
    ISBN-10: 0–8225–6593–5 (lib. bdg. : alk. paper)
    1. Mirra, Dave, 1974– 2. Cyclists—United States—Biography. 3. Bicycle motocross. I. Title.
GV1051.M57S28 2007
796.6092—dc22 [B]   2006019401

Manufactured in the United States of America
1 2 3 4 5 6 – DP – 12 11 10 09 08 07

TABLE OF CONTENTS

GOING FOR GOLD

Dave Mirra soared high in the air on his gold bicycle. He gripped the handlebars and lifted off of his seat. He kicked the bike's frame and sent it spinning beneath him. Dave looked down at the course below. The frame swung back around and underneath him. Dave sat down just before his wheels hit the ground. He had just done a cool 360 tailwhip.

Dave was competing in the 2005 Summer X Games in Los Angeles, California. He was battling nine other stunt riders in the **BMX freestyle park** finals. A park course is jammed with ramps, rails, and boxes. Dave and the other riders each had between 60 and 75 seconds to perform as many wild tricks as possible.

BMX is short for bicycle motocross. BMX bikes have small, 20-inch wheels and small frames. In BMX freestyle, riders perform tricks on ramps, jumps, railings, and other objects.

Judges award points for the tricks. The rider with the most points wins the **gold medal.** Dave had more wins than anyone else in X Games history. A year earlier, he had won his 18th medal. This topped the record of superstar skateboarder Tony Hawk.

Dave's shiny bike wasn't just painted gold for these games. It was actually dipped in real gold. Dave had paid $7,500 for his new bike. "I was hoping I would get to sit on my gold bike while wearing a gold medal around my neck," he said.

A special camera shows Dave performing all the stages of a backflip tailwhip at the 2005 X Games.

Dave fell during this run at the 2005 X Games.

Two days earlier, Dave had tried for first place in a different event. But in the **vert** finals, he had crashed and injured his head. Most fans wondered if he would be able to compete in the park event. Yet here he was, laying out a great run of tricks.

His final trick was a **flipwhip** over the **spine.**
He roared up the ramp and sailed high. Then he
yanked on both handlebars and went into a
backflip. Still in midair, he kicked the bike
around in a tailwhip. He straightened out and
landed cleanly. His score of 89.33 flashed on the
scoreboard. Dave's 19th medal at the X Games
would be gold. It would match his bike! "Last
night I wasn't going to ride," Dave said. "But
there are a lot of
cool and great
fans here. I did it
all for the fans."

This high-flying trick won
Dave the gold medal.

Dave was born in Syracuse, New York.

THROWING TRICKS

David Michael Mirra was born April 4, 1974, in Syracuse, New York. He grew up in nearby Chittenango. Dave's father, Mike, was a TV repairman. Dave's mom, Linda, worked in a hospital. Dave also has an older brother, Tim.

As a kid, Dave loved riding bicycles. He was popping wheelies by the age of five. A year later, he was jumping over garbage cans. He and Tim built ramps with spare wood and cement blocks.

At age eight, Dave rode his first BMX bike. He liked the way he could control this smaller bike. He learned to go off jumps and twist his bike in midair. In 1984, 10-year-old Dave saw his first BMX freestyle competition. He was hooked.

Dave played tennis and basketball for fun. "I tried baseball," he said, "but it was too slow." Dave was more serious about riding.

Sometimes he practiced at a nearby skatepark. "The first time I managed to ride in on an eight-foot quarter-pipe, I couldn't believe it," he said. "I was the happiest dude in the world."

Sometimes Dave let his riding get in the way of his schoolwork. He remembers one teacher making fun of him for always talking about bikes. "He made fun of me," Dave said. "He told me I'd never go anywhere on a bike."

Dave's teacher was wrong. Dave was going places—and fast. By the age of 13, Dave was throwing **big air** tricks at the park.

Dave does a trick in 1989.

Meanwhile, the sport of BMX was becoming popular. Sometimes **professional** riders would pass through Dave's town. Some of the riders noticed Dave's talent. "He had the skills," said BMX superstar Dennis McCoy. "I remember thinking, do I really want to show Dave this trick I've been working on the last few months? He might have it [figured out] by the weekend."

BMX superstar Dennis McCoy *(left)* was impressed with Dave's talent.

In 1992, Dave turned pro. He was just 18 years old. Haro Bikes became his first **sponsor**. Later that year, Dave entered a big vert competition at Daytona Beach, Florida. The best riders in the world were there. They included nine-time world champion Mat Hoffman. Dave shocked everyone by winning the event. A new BMX star had been born. But Dave's career—and his life—almost ended a few months later.

A terrible accident nearly brought Dave's career to an end.

RISING UP

Getting massive air and throwing tricks is dangerous. By the age of 19, Dave had suffered many injuries. But his worst crash happened when he was crossing the street. In December 1993, Dave was run over by a drunk driver. He suffered a head injury and a separated shoulder.

The injuries were serious. "It was pretty gnarly, a near-death kind of thing," said Dave. Dave spent six months healing. Doctors told him he should never get on a BMX bike again. But the whole time, Dave was coming up with ideas for new tricks. "I knew I was riding again, even if it killed me," he said. "Riding is part of me. If I'm still alive, I'm going to do it."

Early in 1995, Dave joined his brother Tim in Greenville, North Carolina. Dave moved into an apartment next to a BMX park. He and Tim rode together. Dave practiced old tricks and invented new ones.

That summer, ESPN created the X Games. Dave entered the vert competition. He competed against the best riders in the world. He took second place—the silver medal. He was thrilled to be fully recovered from his serious injuries.

Later that year, Dave was riding in a state fair in Dallas, Texas. He made a mistake. His shirt got tangled in the handlebars. Dave slammed hard to the ground. Next thing he knew, he was riding in an ambulance. Doctors were working on his broken hand. Dave complained of stomach pains. He had to have surgery.

Smart riders like Dave know how dangerous bike tricks can be. That is why competitors always wear protective gear like helmets and knee and elbow pads. "No matter how cool you think you are," says Dave, "safety gear is a must."

Two months later, Dave was back on his bike again. He kept pushing to learn new and better tricks. He competed at the 1996 X Games in two events—vert and **street**. In vert, he soared to second place. But he won gold in the street event!

Nothing could keep Dave down. Over the next three years, he won X Games gold in both street and vert. He even teamed up with another rider to win gold in vert doubles. He was doing amazing **fufanus**, **X-up flips** over the spine, and big **540s**. His thin body was amazingly strong. "I was doing some pretty burly stuff for a little guy," he said. Dave won nearly every BMX competition. His amazing tricks earned him a new nickname—Miracle Boy.

Dave shows off for fans at a demonstration in New Zealand.

BREAKING RECORDS

As the greatest BMX rider in the world, Dave became rich. In 1999, he earned $400,000 in **prize money** and **endorsements**. He lived in a big house in Greenville with his cat, Simba. Dave began collecting cool cars, including a shiny white Chevrolet Corvette convertible. In his garage, he also kept several Dave Mirra signature Haro bikes.

Dave knows it's important to be smart when you ride. "There is a time to take a risk and a time to chill out," says Dave. "If you're not feeling your best, take the day off and come back the next day."

For the 2000 X Games, Dave decided to pull off a new trick. No rider had ever pulled the double flip in competition. Dave had done it in practice. But this would be his first time doing it at an event.

Dave hit the box and soared 20 feet in the air. Cameras flashed as he did two full circles in the air before landing safely. The crowd exploded with cheers. He won the gold medal again, of course.

Two years later, Dave threw a perfect 540 tailwhip to win another X Games gold. He also won medals at the Global X Games, the Gravity Games, and the Vans Triple Crown of BMX. Dave had been on top for a long time. Was he getting bored? Reporters asked Dave if winning even felt special anymore. "It's always special," he said.

At the 2004 X Games, Dave won gold in both vert and park again. By doing so, he topped

skateboarder Tony Hawk in career X Games medals. Dave had 18 medals, including 13 gold.

Dave performs at the 2004 X Games in Los Angeles, California.

Dave won his record-setting medal in style. He pulled an incredible backflip drop-in. He pedaled out to the edge of the ramp. Then he popped a wheelie into the air and flipped backward as he dropped. "I flipped and saw the ramp," he said, "and I was like, 'Man, I can't believe how good this is working out.'"

Dave *(center)* celebrates his 18th gold medal at the 2004 X Games.

Dave shows off his skills in the half-pipe during a competition.

TRYING HIS BEST

For years, Dave has been the world's most famous BMX freestyle rider. Companies named their bubble gum, shoes, sunglasses, and action figures after him. His *Dave Mirra Freestyle BMX* video game has sold more than a million copies.

In 2004 and 2005, Dave hosted the MTV show *The Inferno*. He appeared on television shows such as *Las Vegas* and *The George Lopez Show*. Dave enjoys being on TV. But it's not the most important thing in his life. "I'm not doing tricks for the recognition or the money," he said. "I just love to ride."

Dave broke his hand again in early 2005. But he soon came back to win his 19th and 20th X Games medals on his 24-karat gold bike. "The bike got way more attention than I did," he said, laughing. "It's so rare and different."

Dave knows that fans expect him to win. Sometimes he feels the pressure. "Because of the success that I've had, I have to live up to certain expectations," he says. "I feel pressure from sponsors and fans who have watched and supported me. I just keep trying my best."

That year, Dave also won an ESPY award as the Best Male Action Sports Athlete. Fans across the country cast more votes for Dave than any other action sports athlete. "Of all the awards that I've won, this is the ultimate compliment," he said. "Because this came from the fans."

Dave arriving at the ESPY Awards in 2005

Dave and Lauren Blackwell married in 2006.

Dave hosts a charity golf tournament each year to raise money for children with serious illnesses. He gives the money to the Dream Factory. It's an organization that makes childrens' dreams come true.

In 2006, Dave started his own BMX bike company, MirraCo. He also married his longtime girlfriend, Lauren Blackwell. Dave was looking forward to winning more X Games medals that summer. But he had a serious injury in practice. Dave was forced to miss the event.

Dave practices old tricks and invents new ones at the Warehouse. The Warehouse is a large building with a vert ramp and a park course with foam pits. Dave rides for three or four hours each day. "It's my own private playground," he says. "I can ride whenever I want, rain or shine." Sometimes Dave invites friends like Ryan Nyquist to the Warehouse for a group practice.

Dave *(right)* is good friends with BMX biker Ryan Nyquist *(left)*.

Dave lifts weights every day and practices tricks in the Warehouse for three to four hours a day.

Dave also lifts weights for two hours a day. "If you're not strict about training, it's going to show," says Dave. "You've got to try your hardest, or don't even bother competing. My goal is to try my best. I don't want to sit on a ramp and go, 'Man, I should have been riding harder.' I know I can't win every single time. Nobody is perfect. Just ride your best and have the best attitude you can."

Selected Career Highlights

2006 Started his own BMX bike company, MirraCo
Finished second in the 2006 Toronto Metro Jam

2005 Won Summer X Games gold medal in BMX park course
Won Summer X Games silver medal in BMX vert best trick
competition

2004 Won Summer X Games gold medal in BMX vert ramp
Won Summer X Games gold medal in BMX park course
Broke record for most medals won in the X Games

2003 Won gold medal in Global X Games BMX park course
Won bronze medal in Global X Games BMX vert ramp
Won silver medal in park course at the Vans Triple Crown of BMX,
Denver, Colorado
Won gold medal in BMX park course at the Montpellier Nokia FISE
competition in Montpellier, France
Won gold medal in BMX vert ramp at the Montpellier Nokia FISE
competition in Montpellier, France

2002 Won Summer X Games gold medal in BMX vert ramp
Won Gravity Games gold medal in BMX park course
Won Gravity Games silver medal in BMX vert ramp

2001 Won Summer X Games gold medal in BMX vert ramp
Won second place in BMX street course at the Vans Triple Crown of
BMX, in Salt Lake City, Utah

2000 Won Summer X Games gold medal in BMX park course
Won Summer X Games silver medal in BMX vert ramp

1999 Won Summer X Games gold medals in BMX street course and in
BMX vert ramp

1998 Won Summer X Games gold medals in BMX street course, BMX vert
ramp, and vert ramp doubles

1997 Won Summer X Games gold medals in BMX street course and in
BMX vert ramp

1996 Won Summer X Games gold medal in BMX street course
Won Summer X Games silver medal in BMX vert ramp

1995 Won Summer X Games silver medal in BMX vert ramp

Glossary

big air: very high off the ground

BMX freestyle park: a competition in which riders perform tricks on a course with ramps, railings, and other obstacles. Park competitions are often called street events.

endorsements: money paid to riders in exchange for promoting a product

540s: tricks where the rider spins the bike one and a half times around and then lands on the half-pipe

flipwhip: a trick that combines a backflip with a tailwhip. To do a tailwhip, the rider makes the bike do a complete spin around the front end of the bike.

fufanus: tricks in which riders go up a ramp, touch the back tire on the edge of the ramp, turn around, and ride down the ramp going forward

gold medal: a prize for winning a competition. The silver medal goes to the second-place finisher. Third place receives bronze.

prize money: money awarded to riders based on their finish in an event

professional: a rider who is allowed to receive prize money for competing. Becoming a professional is also called turning pro.

spine: the top deck of two quarter-pipes placed side to side

sponsor: a company that gives a rider money or equipment

street: a competition in which riders perform tricks on a course with ramps, railings, and other obstacles. Street competitions are often called park events.

vert: a competition on the U-shaped half-pipe. Riders soar above the deck to perform tricks in air.

X-up flips: two tricks in the air—an X-up and a flip. For an X-up, the rider turns the handlebars as far as they will go, turns them back the other way, then straightens them out. A flip is rotating upside down and returning upright before landing.

Further Reading & Websites

Mahaney, Ian F. *Dave Mirra: BMX Champion*. New York: Rosen Publishing Group, 2005.

Rosenberg, Aaron. *Dave Mirra: BMX Superstar*. New York: Rosen Publishing Group, 2005.

Dave Mirra's Official Freestyle BMX Website
http://www.davemirra.com
Dave's official website features trivia, photos, records, and information about Dave and BMX riding.

EXPN.com
http://expn.go.com
The EXPN website provides extreme sports news, including BMX news.

Sports Illustrated for Kids
http://www.sikids.com
The *Sports Illustrated for Kids* website covers all sports, including BMX riding.

Index

Photo Acknowledgments

The images in this book are used with the permission of: © Jason Merritt/WireImage.com, pp. 4, 22; © Bo Bridges/CORBIS, pp. 6, 27; © Phillip Ellsworth/WireImage.com, p. 7; © Getty Images, pp. 8, 14, 18, 23, 25; © Syracuse Newspapers/David Lassman/The Image Works, p. 9; © Trevor Graves, p. 11; © Shelly Castellano/Icon SMI, p. 12; © Tony Donaldson/Icon SMI, p. 20; AP Images/Mark J. Terrill, p. 21; © Nancy Kaszerman/ZUMA Press, p. 26; AP Images/Gerry Broome, p. 28; © Al Fuchs/NewSport/CORBIS, p. 29.

Front Cover: © Vaughn Youtz/ZUMA Press